T0209733

BEING LOVE

Haiku and Art to Awaken Your Heart

SHANI

BALBOA.
PRESS

A DIVISION OF HAY HOUSE

Balboa Press books may be ordered through booksellers or by contacting:

Balboa Press
A Division of Hay House
1663 Liberty Drive
Bloomington, IN 47403
www.balboapress.com
1 (877) 407-4847

Because of the dynamic nature of the Internet, any web addresses or links contained in this book may have changed since publication and may no longer be valid. The views expressed in this work are solely those of the author and do not necessarily reflect the views of the publisher, and the publisher hereby disclaims any responsibility for them.

The author of this book does not dispense medical advice or prescribe the use of any technique as a form of treatment for physical, emotional, or medical problems without the advice of a physician, either directly or indirectly. The intent of the author is only to offer information of a general nature to help you in your quest for emotional and spiritual well-being. In the event you use any of the information in this book for yourself, which is your constitutional right, the author and the publisher assume no responsibility for your actions.

Print information available on the last page.

ISBN: 978-1-9822-2045-7 (sc)
ISBN: 978-1-9822-2044-0 (hc)
ISBN: 978-1-9822-2046-4 (e)

Library of Congress Control Number: 2019900845

Balboa Press rev. date: 07/01/2019

BEING LOVE

Haiku and Art to Awaken Your Heart

PRAYER

May all beings be Liberated

May all beings know the Truth

May all beings be blessed by Love

Om Shanti, Shanti, Shanti

I bow to Supreme

Holy Creator of all

Keep me close to You

Water drips weightless

Raindrops on my window sill

God's touch as water

Oh heart of all hearts

Warm my being with fire

You are my true love

Beloved is truth

Love is singular wholeness

I am That I am

Rest your soul in peace

The ego dies before death

I am one with God

Prophecy's kisses

Love does not tell any lies

Truth always abides

Glittering brightly

Chandra, the God of soma

You are pure white light

Buddha's silent gaze

Empty and still, sweet and soft

Buddha's silent heart

Holy Spirit loves

Eternally and freely

You are Holy Love

Sita and Rama

Melted in Love's communion

The Divine union

Amrita's sweet scent

Fills my heart with endless joy

Beloved's warm kiss

Love's luscious blessings

Overflows within my soul

I now dance naked

God's holy spirit

Grace flows endlessly in love

Great blessings to you

Resting in my Self

Union with God, I am That

I am That I am

Birth, death, love, hate, One

End, beginning, all is One

Light, dark, sun, moon, One

Empty in Thy will

My seeking eyes are shut still

Love's kiss is my will

Closed heart, full of pain

Blocks God's true reality

Pray for Truth and Love

Light as a feather

Floating weightlessly and free

Flying on Truth's wings

Mahasatta Om

I worship Great existence

Shakti Om Shakti

Let love be the guide

Open your heart, close your eyes

Love is God's compass

I am in the field

You are the field and contents

Praise Almighty One

Divine Satguru

My heart blessed with truth by You

Divine Satguru

My love is so still

Silence gives me a deep thrill

I rest in Thy will

Body, nobody

Nobody sees absolute

Nobody is truth

Hate separation

Always be one with the Truth

The way of no way

Abide in my soul

You exist where eyes don't see

Known Reality

Surya, the sun God

Light illuminating love

Shine your light on me

You love just to be

Infinite love sets me free

Grace deep as the sea

Divine mother God

Paravati's Love shines bright

I bow to Mother

Green Tara dancing

Goddess mesmerizing light

Amrita flowing

Infinite lotus

My closed heart is now open

Flying free in love

I slay vicious thoughts

My mind's tricks are all unreal

The grand illusion

The heart is the guide

This mind is no friend of mine

Love's absolute prize

Cleanse your mental wounds

Let light enter and be free

Be cleansed from karma

Arunachala

You are Shiva's holy light

Arunachala

I Bow to Shiva

You are the great destroyer

I am merged with You

Omnipresent One

Rid me of all arrogance

Shine your light on me

God's hide and seek play

Leela will lead you astray

Love is where to stay

Dream within a dream

Illusions made by your thoughts

I pray to be Home

Who is in control?

What's perceived reality?

What will be will be.

Silent awakened

My heart sings beauty and joy

My home is stillness

Asleep in the dream

All I see is ignorance

Now time to wake up

I bow to Vishnu

You preserve the Divine will

Oh almighty One

Blooming lotuses

Om mani padhme hum Om

Jeweled spirit loves

Dancing emptiness

I am innocent beauty

I am That I am

Shining golden light

I am purified Unborn

Free from birth and death

Omnipotent One

Shiva Shiva Shiva Om

Omnipresent One

Rhada and Krishna

Union as the Beloved

Seen as Love's pure heart

Wisdom is knowing

Love is power of being

Truth is objectless

Your love is so true

Deep colors of royal blue

I bow to Saturn

Gratitude I am

No more person attitude

Love and Truth I am

Sacred Beloved

Your grace flies high up above

Love fits like a glove

Bow to Arjuna

Krishna's golden heart I am

Divine by nature

Words do not bring peace

Silence fills the heart with ease

Resting unborn heart

God is the doer

I am only a paintbrush

The canvas is Love

Who am I? I am

What am I? I am Divine

Who am I? I am

Oh, Almighty One

I absorb myself in You

Life dissolves in You

Golden eagle sees

The inner eye shines brightly

Soaring free with Love

Life is not our own

No past or present exists

All Oneness persists

Beyond what we see

No time, space, reality

Truth is what will be

Attachment binds us

Detached from reality

Truth will set us free

I bow to Saturn

Your love blesses all with truth

Self-importance dies

Hail oh mighty One

Love's all-pervading essence

Radiates my heart

The open secret

Is free for all ears to hear

Listen intently

Mahakriya Om

I worship the Great doer

Shakti Om Shakti

Made in God's image

Illusions are washed away

I am That I am

Atman, soul's driver

Your mind is a false driver

Stay empty and free

Don't keep me apart

I melt as one with your heart

Love is a new start

It is what it is

It's the end of the story

To be or not be

Vayu, the wind God

Sweet blows of love through the air

Moves infinitely

Now open your ears

Now time to open your eyes

You are love Divine

Separation lies

Stop the false reality

Illusion not bliss

Do you think you are

Mind, body, soul, thinking thoughts

Love, God, Self, Nothing

You do not exist

Illusory thoughts will lie

Who or what are you?

Do not please the mind

Empty lover you will find

Beloved is kind

Released from prison

Released from separation

Free from time and space

Standing or sitting

Questioning or answering

Do or be nothing

Sacredness dancing

Divine's infinite prayers

Void of all objects

Your mentor is Love

Your heart's compass sees the Truth

This guide won't deceive

Love's mighty hero

Not bound by separation

Rejoice in freedom

Brahman, I am That

Infinite freedom and truth

Liberated soul

Rhibu always sees

He doesn't hide truth from me

Rhibu set me free

Sit, do, be, or stand

Mind games like a poker hand

Nothing wins the prize

Infinite dreamer

I am one, Para Brahman

No separation

I bow to Indra

The sacred God to the sky

Darkness defeated

God's love flowering

Fountain of truth overflows

I am now at Home

Sweet butterfly kiss

Drinking loves endless nectar

Love joyous and sweet

Be still and know that

I am God, I am alone

I am Love and Truth

Sri Ganesha Om

I bow to Divine within

Bless me with your Grace

I pray Satguru

Free my mind from illusion

Melt in love with me

I am Lord Shiva

I free you from illusion

I am One with you

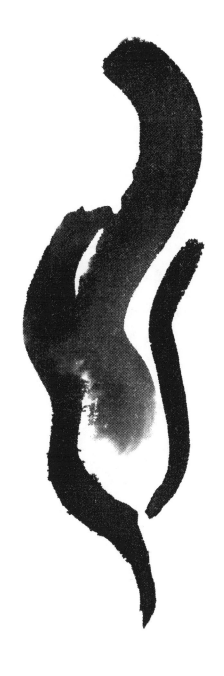

You are what you are

Everything is and will be

Unification

Mind made up concepts

Conclusions are illusions

Your thoughts hide the Truth

You, me, I, he, she

Is this your reality?

Discover the truth

Love, Truth, Empty, Still

Free from thoughts becomes God's will

Peace, Silence, Presence

Soul is always new

Lose your thoughts that stick like glue

Present living you

Love greater than skies

Kill all of my ego's lies

Your truth is so wise

Holy Amrita

Loves essence sweet as honey

I am bathed in God

Holy candles flame

Illuminating the Truth

Know thyself as God

No self-existence

Live in the absolute void

Here the truth resides

Relax and be free

Let go, what will be will be

Perfect harmony

Free from samsara

Your identity chains leave

Emptiness dancing

Let your heart shine bright

Radiant liberation

Being true and free

One reality

Everything is and will be

What will be will be

Wisdom healing love

Soul is cleansed with holy light

Released from bondage

I have a secret

Do not believe any thoughts

Love's divine essence

Naked dance with God

Flying freely in heaven

Heaven is on earth

Unknown mystery

Wisdom hidden in your heart

Beloved shining

SHANI

www.greatblessingoftruth.com

Shani is an American spiritual teacher who delivers the simple message: "Know Thyself." Her books are invitations to inquire into the heart of your being so that you may experience a life filled with love and peace, free from suffering. She is also the author of *Whispers of Grace.*

Printed in the United States
By Bookmasters